All I Can Recall
PAUL GENEGA

salmonpoetry

Published in 2013 by
Salmon Poetry
Cliffs of Moher, County Clare, Ireland
Website: www.salmonpoetry.com
Email: info@salmonpoetry.com

Copyright © Paul Genega, 2013

ISBN 978-1-908836-42-7

All rights reserved. No part of this publication may be reproduced or transmitted in any form or by any means, electronic or mechanical, including photography, recording, or any information storage or retrieval system, without permission in writing from the publisher. The book is sold subject to the condition that it shall not, by way of trade or otherwise, be lent, resold or otherwise circulated without the publisher's prior consent in any form of binding or cover other than that in which it is published and without a similar condition, including this condition, being imposed on the subsequent purchaser.

COVER ARTWORK: "Pie" © Aaron Fink. Reproduced by kind permission of the artist.
COVER DESIGN: *Siobhán Hutson*

Printed in Ireland by Sprint Print

Acknowledgements

Grateful acknowledgement is made to the following publications in which these poems (sometimes in earlier incarnations) first appeared:

AT THE TONE (Three Mile Harbor Press): *Out Takes*

COLORADO-NORTH REVIEW: *Parentheses*

ELECTR! *Elegy for Pollock*

HOME PLANET NEWS: *Working Life, The Kaddish Was Finished, Gardenia Castlehill, Macrowaves* (under the title *The Collapse of Communism*)

NEW YORK QUARTERLY: There are Eight Million Stories

PATERSON LITERARY REVIEW: *The Great Depression*

SALMON: A JOURNEY IN POETRY 1981 – 2007: *Wolfie's Tavern*

SKY ANTHOLOGY: *Boring Alice*

STILLWATER REVIEW: *Stephen Duck, Tragedy*

Contents

The Great Depression	11
Man of War: 1942	14
Boring Alice	17
The Ed Sullivan Show	19
Out Takes	21
Five Paragraph Essay	23
Macrowaves	26
Working Life	27
There are Eight Million Stories	29
Communion	32
Gardenia Castlehill	33
Upper West Side, Oregon	34
Wolfie's Tavern	36
The Kaddish Was Finished	38
Dover Sole	40
Reliquary	42
Husband: Man of War 2002	49
Toast	51

From the Catalogues	59
Scottish Opera	60
Stephen Duck	62
Elegy for Pollock	64
Parentheses	67
Tragedy	68
After a Phone Call	69
About the Author	75

THE GREAT DEPRESSION

In the Brooklyn deli during the Depression
she did what deli owners did,
packed up food and sent her son – my father –
to parcel out to neighbors on relief.

Ukrainian neighbors, one presumes, got more,
just a slice of sausage more,
dollop of potato salad, extra pickle.

Not that she had much except for the store,
a husband in the rail yards, a fine frail pale son
dying beneath blankets embossed *Pensy*,
another who survived and did what he was told.

She had Genghis Kahn cheekbones
and smelled like boiled cabbage.

From the look of grainy sepias
she was never young, not ever.

Esprit, though, she had plenty,
esprit and solidarity with
those who were her people,
those who prayed and sang like home.

Her eyes were quick
but her worries were deep –
the fir forest of a folk tale where
she sat in a mud floor wood shack.

It was in those years, the deli years,
she perfected her egg bread
famous fifty Easters hence,
contracted wishbone-leg arthritis,
learned enough English
to read Winchell and *The Eagle*

On this day in that life
she stands behind the counter
in a leather smock marked *Dilbert's*,
a gift from a friend who works
the late night shift at Dilbert's.

The unsmiling Americans
have banned booze in their country
so she has done what deli owners did —
mixed hooch in the back
to sell out of brown paper bags.

A man orders a ham sandwich
and she makes him one, a good one,
piled high with plenty of fat.
He gets three tins of macaroni,
cole slaw, coffee, pickles.

It's a big sale, a good day

until, squinting, winking, he asks…
if… as he has heard, he
might get… you know… schnapps.

This man is not a neighborhood man
but he's courteous, knows the tongue.

In one ear the voice of reason,
voice which knows this is the law,
knows with complete clarity what is to occur.
In the other, prayer and song,
her people, the hope she has to sail.

She hands him a bottle.
He slaps on the cuffs.

And though she lived another five plus decades
and could sing tales all day long,
this one she never sang.

This one she kept
in a mud floor forest hovel
where only she could go
to explain again to wind
and other unsmiling powers
how much those damned medicines cost.

MAN OF WAR: 1942

The waves that first time in Florida
were warm as Jones Beach in July
but this was February, rising falling
two stories high and higher
lolling rolling sweeping as he'd been swept
off hard time streets by Hitler
FDR and Churchill, the churn
and burn of worlds blared black and white
in headlines read and reread
enough that he'd enlisted
shipped not to high seas –
Sicily, Samoa, Pago Pago, St. Lo –
but a prime patch of ritz, West Palm Beach
him all of 22, stutteringly thick
tongued, Bushwick born and bred
not at all he knew a matinee Apollo
though he was trying, yes was trying

dolphin dipping
in white water
back flip breast
stroke cartwheel kick cavorting
for four fair
socialites on shore, each demurely staring
at a glass of cuba libre, canapé
of watercress, lime slice, 'nilla wafer

Dear Lord he thought them lovely
and he was happy, hungry happy
going out, out

of the shallows, out beyond the whip surf
where blue balloons bobbed
atop the waves, like the powdered wigs
of loreleis, lace
brassieres of sea sprites
he simply had to touch
caress, brush across his brow

him now stroking hard, hurled high
into the dazzle, towards the blue dreams
of the sea, just a second splash
away, and for once him feeling
proud, despite garlicky father
bashfulness and poverty, ignorance of politics
war plans or politenesses
this one time feeling proud, nearly pirouetting
shoreward to show off
to the damsels his manly derring-do

and they did see, yes they saw
all four springing to their feet
hooting shrieking screaming
flailing their alabaster arms
no longer loathsome
Private First Class he'd become
a hero, warrior pursuer of oceanic pleasure
a man of war, the Man

except except
and in his mind's eye only this
would later matter, instead what he saw
was them waving him west

back onto the beach, back to army
blanket, to cabana, to self
back, they cried, back back
so back he swam, back back
away from the blue bobbers
from his mermaids' mesh mantillas
from the single crackerjack of courage
he had mustered, from a beauty so innocent
and basic it can sting, from a war story
he could someday tell a son
without feeling ashamed

BORING ALICE

I had seen the army whistle with its worn white star,
had heard how The City, fright-wigged New York City,
faded to black when the civil defense men trilled,
how the night was X'd by beacons
and the good, far away, had rained fire on the bad:

that was the sky before I was born, not long before
and an age. Over the new roofs of Long Island
there was moon – there, sun – each where it belonged,
occasionally an aeroplane tilting into Idlewild,
low brief rumbles then back to the quiescent façade.

In those domesticated heavens, horrors
had to be found. Tabloids served up saucers
of one-horned green-clawed Martians,
winged things grew large as schoolyards,
slumbering hungers stretched and arose.

Surely a quiet sky was preferable.
And so we had the preferable sunset to dawn
seven days a week that whole decade.
Except for the summer when the atmosphere
conspired a miracle, of sorts.

My father, a shy man who had
blown the wartime whistle and in peace
built fighter planes, packed me in the Chevy
and drove us one night to the beach.
We were going to see what God hath brought

all the way from the North Pole.
Strange, I remember, to see the Sound so dark.
The sand felt cool, nice as a fresh pillow.
We walked quickly, unswervingly, wordlessly
towards waves. Then precisely at the tide line

father spun me around and screamed *look!*
There on the horizon was a line of dancing lilac,
a purple pulse, a quivering… *Wow! O Wow!*
I stammered, as if he were responsible
and above all, had to be spared.

A roar of boring Alice, all the way
from the North Pole —

in a world of half-healed bruises
just another
which seemed to belong.

THE ED SULLIVAN SHOW

for my generation

Shock still in wingback chairs,
one eye watched the window for snow,
a sudden squall to deliver us from Monday,

the knotting sense that this was it
forever – tedious series of locking obligations,
bridges spanning bridges, highways feeding highways,
ad infinitum, excelsior, et. al.

This ritual, this hour, this flickering
imagery – beautiful, bathetic – was more
than entertainment, more than passing time.

The man with shrug shoulders and loose suits
was our Virgil, our square, self-conscious courier
of Culture –

    fleet sleek Russian swans
    septets of somersaulting siblings
    Berlin drummed on twin washboards
    poodles jumping hoops of fire
    big grin farm boy singing
    Mimi's death and Carmen's
    a Noah's ark of stars.

Outside the stars, distant and commanding,
insisted tomorrow the yellow bus would come
and off we'd go to split shifts of memorize,
repeat —

    capitals, hypotenuses, Cyrano, amoebae —

what else could we do except sink into the cushions,
what else have we done except get on with the show?

OUT TAKES

Alternative endings, reshot scenes, extra footage —
much is lost on the cutting room floor,
unspliced to the feature we view fixed,
almost inevitable, no matter how flawed.

Sometimes we can sense it —

trench-coated Bogart
freezes the propellers
to have his gauzy love

dart-eyed Cary Grant
lets beloved *monkey face*
slip into the abyss.

But there are secrets we would not guess —

fright-wigged Swanson
flailing down the stairs
awakes her dreaming son

Welles in death throes
mutters *plums*

yes, plums —
much has been lost
and in the losing, much gained.

Clark Gable, ripping down
the blanket, plops on top
a rapt Claudette Colbert

Brando blubs to Steiger
I could have been a contender
instead of a Christ figure
which is what I am

Would we have loved Paul Henreid more
if he lit five stogies at once
and danced with a lampshade on his head?

Why ask for the moon
when we already have such stars?

O golden stars –

Janet Leigh finishes her shower
drives penitent to Phoenix
with a surprise in the back seat

Dummont guns down her tormentors

A Gish runs away with the groom.

Accident, pratfall, forgotten line, sneeze,
what did and did not occur –

him opening his arms
as I run gaily towards him
whispering over and over *you are loved.*

FIVE PARAGRAPH ESSAY

for all the poets teaching English 101

The house had the sad feel of past glory –
chipped paint, broken windows, parquet floors
incised with penknives, servant staircase
missing treads – but also six bedrooms,
an enormous parlor with boarded up hearth,
formal dining room with pocket doors,
more than enough space to host some
of the throng expected in Washington to protest
the unending war. Two groups were assigned us,
one from Harvard, the other SUNY Buffalo;
it could have been Andromeda and Mars.

To begin with the signature of life in 1970:
the way they smoked marijuana.
The Buffalo contingent grabbed a joint
from your hand the second it was lit,
then thrust it to confreres, all the while
spewing smoke like backfiring pickups.
By the time you could mumble
mind passing it here? or don't mind if I do
it was time to find a roach clip
to suck the last sputtering life out of the nub.
The Harvard folk, in contrast, puffed
quickly then immediately passed underhand
to the right, as if half expecting the Feds
to burst in. And like my fellow Hoya,
that year a Rhodes Scholar at Oxford,
they seemed never to inhale.

And then the way they cursed.
The Buffalo gang made sure to use
some form of *fuck* in every sentence
uttered, as in *Fuck this fucking country
and the fucked up fucking mess
the fuckers have fucked us with.*
Harvard usage was more sparing
and leaned toward the non-sequitur,
as in *The American people do not
yet understand that this is a civil war
which the US has no business meddling in,
nor do they understand that this
unconstitutional military adventurism
is eroding resources required for
education, transportation, housing
and other absolute essentials.
Until we can communicate this clearly
there will be hurt and misunderstanding
on both sides of the political divide
and I don't give a fuck what father says.*

But the most vivid contrast could be seen
on the morning of the march. Buffalo emerged
surprisingly early given the late night debauch,
all ten bounding downstairs adorned in red
bandanas, combat boots and gas masks,
skeins of metal chains in-hand, determined
to confront porcine violence head-on.
The Harvard men and Radcliffe women,
on the other hand, after long showers
and numerous cups of black coffee
donned ties and dresses (respectfully).

They would skip the march entirely
and head instead for the Hill, certain,
it seemed, that once Crimson opinion
was known, all problems foreign
and domestic would be solved.

I wouldn't say I much liked either group.
No one bothered to thank us when they left.
No one made a bed or threw out the trash.
No one offered a dime for food consumed
or dope blown. Yes, they were both rotten,
as far as I was concerned – self-absorbed,
delusional and breathtakingly impolite.
And yet, if truth be told, it was that day
on the Mall I tasted acrid tear gas
the first time and I must report
for the sake of historical accuracy:
that fucker fucking stang.

MACROWAVES

In that magazine office, early 1970's, we were
mostly recent grads. I was a Ph.D.
dropout. Bruce was slightly older,
absurdly handsome (he wanted to model).
Once he got a call back. Turned out,
they liked his hands. Those hands he used
like the rest of us to pound out copy
telling retailers what to sell and how.
Mainly we rewrote press releases or else
we made stuff up. One poor guy in Kansas
said he'd sold Amanas at our recommended price
and had gone bust in a week. The job forever
ruined me on capitalism. It also ruined my liver
(martinis after work). We were a small staff,
arrogantly precocious and casually incestuous.
All except Bruce. He went for older men
with carousel horses in Connecticut farm houses.
Or else he went to the baths. The Divine Miss M
was singing there back then. It really was
long, long ago. But I've been thinking about
Bruce lately with the collapse of communism
and the rise of the American Right.
I've been thinking about the last lead he wrote
for an article about ovens – *if reports can be
believed, micros are the waves of the future* –
before he barricaded himself in his apartment
and refused to answer the phone. I never
got to see Bruce again, never got to tell him
he had the pulse of something in those words.
I quit myself a month later. At the exit
interview I told Human Resources,
The problem is I'm socialist. I meant it too.
It seemed, as it seems, the wave of the future.

WORKING LIFE

> *The worker puts his life into the object,*
> *and his life then belongs no longer to*
> *himself but to the object.*
>
> KARL MARX

When this boy puts on Marilyn,
Honey, call it love. Saturday
down in Asbury, I played
The Ice Dome (spotlights, glitter,
cardboard drop of Cartier's)
and from the very second I kicked
through the curtain, swept back
the pink silk scarf and started in
with *Diamonds*, they were whistling
and stomping so I could hardly hear
the song. But the time I shook
the boobs and tossed those tags
marked *Tiffany's* out on the tables,
Honey, they were wild. I just pranced
around that stage, showing leg,
some bare ass, something to take
home with them. Later, I downed

three straight Dewars, doubles,
and I was whirling on a bar stool
by closing. That didn't stop me.
I just walked myself to the Ho-Jo,
still dressed. What should I care?
Four in the morning there I am
stepping down the street, right past

two fat cops, them staring and staring.
Four AM in Asbury this dizzy blitzo
Marilyn is tripping down Sea Drive
(me nearly six-two in the pumps).
La Di Da, I say, blow them a kiss,
hike up the dress to my thighs.
I didn't care. Them staring and
staring. Me in such a rush. See,

this man I'd met, this good man,
this decent man, this man, he'd
promised to come over, so I sat down
at the mirror, brushed the hair,
slipped on thicker lashes. Then
I practiced pouting and holding
my knees the way she did. I powdered
all over, poured another double
with lots of fine crushed ice and
did my lips. I was itching to undress,
slip on a tee and jeans, but knew
I couldn't. See, when I put on
Marilyn, my lover-man sees stars,
but shit… he just gets sick
when I play… me.

THERE ARE EIGHT MILLION STORIES

After a night of bath house sex,
about as spent as a 22 year old gets,
I whistled up Broadway, salt bagel
in hand, steam cleaned, feeling good.

A few Off Duty taxis slo-moed past,
trawling for white fares.
The first Korean grocer
was unshuttering her shop.
A mountain of stained burlap
snored against a door.

Otherwise, just me. The city
which never sleeps was sleeping
and I was the tired, happy hero
of my sweetly tawdry life,

hooking west on a cross street in the 80's
drowsing my way home
when suddenly – from nowhere –
a cruiser careened to my side
and I was awash in cop static, red flares.

Two officers pounced out,
one about 6'2", very early 30's,
sandy hair and mustache,
hazel eyes, lots of time outdoors,
Robert Redford type,
no wedding band,

the other mid-forties Peter Lorre.

Two officers pounced out
pulling out their pistols.
and just like Naked City
I reached for the sky, dropped
the lethal bagel, began
searching for something to confess.

In a flash they had me
spreadeagled on their vehicle,
huge hands patting me down,
reaching under shirt,
tugging at my chest hairs,
rubbing my overly clean skin.

Perhaps after that they spoke to me,
perhaps asked who I was,
where I was going, where I'd been.
Perhaps there was a soundtrack
for the film that I'd been spliced in

but all I can recall is the silent drive
to Riverside, the man on the corner
in the same teal shirt
I had worn the day before
opining with conviction
I was the sniper he had seen.

And how even hours later
after they'd dumped me at my building
and I was quivering under covers
reconfiguring a future, and definitely
deciding Dustin should play me,
I still didn't get their snickers,
their winks and *gotcha* grins,
being O that young and trusting,
that starry-eyed, that dumb.

COMMUNION

for Jim

Later on the ground, one man lost it
believing the baggage had burned –

wailed his grief in glass shattering crescendos,
flailing against the inert empty carousel,

a Rumpelstiltskin czardas of impotence and rage –
but when the cabin first filled with smoke

everyone on board, as if narcotized
by their imminent demise,

eased into an odd collective calm.
If not now, when? I remember thinking

as the smoke thickened forty miles from New York.
Does He exist for you or not? This is it. Decide…

Then turned and asked if you'd care to share
a stick of spearmint, knowing at that moment –

with the heaviest of certitudes – the only one
I wished to talk to was you, my love in the live vile air.

GARDENIA CASTLEHILL

in memory of Marjorie Finnell

Egg yolk silks, wool snoods,
tea leaf shawls, tigress synthetics –
you slipped in and out of selves

believing all the world's one,
sauntered dainty toed at odd hours,
parasol moon held aloft.

Broadway star – cross-street 97th –
voice sultry as an Alabamian afternoon –
trawling yawl with mizzen luffing –

you found lustrous lines in city litter,
the ineffable in Moxie,
and your humor was muscular, like camp.

Lovely, limpid, anything but tawdry,
by the time you found the theater
you had become your own weather –

so fashionably late, your debut
notice noted, not even death
could hold the curtain back.

UPPER WEST SIDE, OREGON

You kept adding bracelets
until your arms were sleeves of silver
clanging louder than the locals
into the fronded café, accent
you were reared with pitched to assault,
flush all with a queasy sense of awe.

A slight sight you were, a flicker-lick of light,
more energy than mass, unabashedly enthused
about the heaping plate of omelets,
extra toast – and biscuits –
you refused to touch, wouldn't even look at.

Gazing out at thin firs,
you asked again if the bagels remained good,
if the new millennium had caught up with knishes,
if quarts of hot and sour could still be had
at dawn while grocers stacked green apples –

place defined by food
and you embodying a memory of place –
edited, distilled, stock, almost cartoonish.

Later on the hiking trail
your high heels negotiated tree roots with aplomb,
stumbling just once, facing off
a black bear in a berry bacchanal.

Your arms sounded. The bear loped away.

But what I remember best is you
standing in the maiden hair
staring down the dark path, leaning over
slightly, willowy, as if waiting
for the IRT to finally carry you home.

WOLFIE'S TAVERN

in memory of Bob Fuchs

Shadow home,
lair, the dark
place your sick
body honed

in on. You ate
verboten burgers
nursed lager,
excuse to pontificate

on the tv news,
to extol, to pronounce,
opine and renounce –
as you would say: schmooze.

What the locals
thought of your
New York jaw,
what the yokels,

as you called
them, felt
about your purpled pelt
cannot be recalled

but at that moment
you were top shelf,
the Alpha wolf,
and you lent

your jejune know-it-all
to the unimpatient masses.
Blotched with rashes,
a thrall

of skin and bone,
you bristled and scowled,
yelp-howled
on your bar throne

as if bluster and bray
could pass for folks talking,
wit's fangs keep stalking
death at bay.

THE KADDISH WAS FINISHED

in memory of Marty Kellman

and there we were on Amsterdam
stunned with the sun as our headlight

and because I loved you so much
I couldn't stop, couldn't stop crying

squall after squall after squall

until the blond big haired
yenta from Student Affairs

(she rumored an expert on affairs)

chastised me to stop,
shot a *you big sissy* look

which for one shocked
second almost worked

sob suddenly retreating
like a mudslide in reverse

then broke again.

There on the asphalt corner
amid litter and carnations

O my mentor, my colleague
my irreplaceable confrere

love proved itself
once again unstoppable

took stock of itself
as the measure of our lives.

DOVER SOLE

On Mother's Day, my mother was sitting
in her high-back, pretending to read the newspaper.
Her eyes were iron skillets glazed with bacon grease.
It looked as if she'd not blinked in many minutes,
some internal clock telling her the time to turn the page.

I watched a few moments, then announced my arrival,
letting the screen door slam. Her head turned and
she said my name, as if surprised to see me, as if
trying to remember who I was supposed to be.

I bent down and kissed the cheek she offered.
The cheek was cold. Even that fine morning
with the windows shut and drapes drawn,
she was cold. And sweating. Wads of crumpled tissues
lay beside a cracked hand mirror she used
to check her teeth and muss her tangled hair.

I took a seat and waited for her to say my sister
had not called. She said it. And then because my father
was not yet back from mass, she got talkative.
The day's sermon was child molestation and
a fisherman in Quogue who lost both feet to a shark.
Freak accidents and depravity were the things
she loved best. And she knew lots – so much, I concluded,
she only pretended to pretend to read the paper.

When my father came home, we shook hands
then he shook martinis. It wasn't quite noon
but we had reservations at a restaurant
lined with Victorian valentines. I filled the stale room
with chatter about work. Father talked golf.
Mother belted hers and quickly asked for more.
Drunk, she cursed, so father said to wait five.

Then we had another round and I gave her a gift
She peeled back festive paper, crumpled it
with Kleenex, and took out an inlaid teak frame.
She stared at it acutely, as if studying a photo
familiar yet unclear, but did not say a word.

She did not say anything the rest of Mother's Day
except *the soup. Dover sole, mashed potatoes,*
peas and double chocolate mud cake
until my sister called at five when she said
the old house was too fucking small for visitors
and never go wading in the dark.

RELIQUARY

Teeth

Chipped, brittle, licorice riddled,
silver-filled, yellowy, yanked.

When you couldn't this or that
or anything, when you claimed
you perspired in gasp-ghastly perfusion,

when Depression era greens
on a Delancey Street pushcart
seemed fresher than the frise on your plate

the teeth were to blame.

Your mother, your model who hated
her uppers, went without –

deleted dentures discovered
months later inside a fondue pot –

but you behind sewn mouth
still wear yours, I presume,

those painful lodgers,
stained xylophones, those ruins –

no baguette, no Gruyere,
no chardonnay, no kirsch,

nothing to chew on but eternity.

Hair

You kept fifty years a box of your ringlets
in the lingerie drawer, along with –
whys unknown – a copy of *Mein Kampf*.

Fraulein of fine blondness
frau dyed shrieking red
you settled for matted gray, unkempt –

your right hand mid-salute
reaching for the forehead,
smashing palm on forehead,

as if the envoy of execrable cries.

Eyes

Blue ice
melting

into pools –

wanting
windows

I'd stare
there

and see
self –

a terrible
terror
of falling

through sky
water

water sky
sky water

down to
the depths

we called
love.

Hands

The fingers right-angled
morphed into your mother's

I wanted a soft touch, grandmother's,
but your hands didn't do that –

they were birds caught in your hair
or they lay in your lap, angry,
waiting for communion without priests.

Mouth

a door,
a car door,
a tiny toy-like car door
on a squat uncolored car
careened into the ring
zig-zagged, doing wheelies

and out popped
a score of clowns
a whole tribe of merry clowns
with rumpjopes, boops and hugles,
a universe of circuses
let-go lollapaloozas

right there at the lawyer's
to everyone's unsmiling awe

Torso

The old women
visited your body –

mud hut, black pot,
centuries of Slavdom –

made you theirs.

They bided their time –

moderne thin at first,
borzoi sleek, twig pretty,
you plumped like a pierogi.

On your unsteady feet they walked
again their first boots on America
swaying with vodka and the sea.

Feet

When you were young and I a child
we'd skate away our Saturdays
on a concrete outdoor rink.

It's the best that we had —

the two of us up on little wheels
going round and round
round round going round —

the park in October a museum diorama,
Kodachrome orange in quickening air —

round round going round
round round going round —

how fast, mother, how fast
it was, from orbit to obit.

Dust

The rag in-hand
and mother tears
always for nothing
would ever come clean

a film unseen
by any eyes but yours.

What a terrible end to become
what you most hated

dust dust dust dust –

dust to dust mother,
dust to dust –

and a son who's too
quick with amens.

HUSBAND: MAN OF WAR 2002

My sister's second. She's taken his name. Must love him lots
to shed Swanson for Stuckenschneider.

First name Jim. Like my partner. Met hers at their wedding
outside Denver. Sis Barbied-up, babooned with mascara.
Nothing demure about her. There never was.

Freights clanked, almost touchable, past the redwood deck
reception. People danced. Drank. Whiffed traces of train diesel.
Everyone and me had big fun.

Jim's an ex-marine. The son of a marine. Grandson
of a marine. His two sons wore dress blues as ushers.

They're strapping boys, Jim's sons. Half-Thai and handsome.
Boisterous and silly. Chugalug grinners who affix
what they think is adulthood on command.

One was packing for Iraq. The other just back from Kuwait.
I keep thinking about them, these newest marines from
a family of marines. The sacrosanct creed, jut-jawed sense
of service, sullied by the bloodlust of a bully boy from Yale.

I keep thinking about their knee jerk dumb luck rite
of passage and of human rights defiled. About their epic warrior
wishes and the open ended, calculated management of fear.
About their Hollywood hormonal high jinx rush at exploit
and the cynic's exploitation of a dark acrid age.

Not Jim nor his granddad nor his father nor his sons would
care much for such musings. Jim was downsized after 9/11.
He's frantic scared of car bombs. But he's never voted
anything but Right. And never will.

And they'd be open mouth aghast at the fantasies I'm having.
To the ones the boys teased with their Chippendale strip
on the deck they'd just yawn. More suspect is this:
a young marine disembarking slips on a slick
and is flown to a cushy plush hospital to recupe.

How desperate my daydreams.

Breaking bones of a uniformed attacker. Putting him in
splints to keep him from harm's way. To spare the smolder
his dangerous obedience. To defuse the lethal rocket
in his pocket. Breaking toes as neatly as the craven
Texanized Caligula broke faith with the nation, body
politic, collective, every American citizen of the world.

How desperate my daydreams. How desperate my brother.

Somewhere now in Basra a man and a woman twine eyes
as they marry. He smiles Jim's smile. She laughs big and brassy.
His two grown sons wear berets and old fatigues.
People dance. Drink tea. A freight train ghosts past.

And we celebrate Eros in death dusted air.

TOAST

It was paunchy Nat the older brother
hair slicked back with tonic
gut girded with Night Watch cummerbund
eyes ablaze like cherries jubilee
who rose with the flute

even though the groom,
the hour's man, the star
who never had forgotten
how he'd flipped him out
of Mantle, Whitey Ford and Mays
not to mention Sandy Koufax
nor his nattering the first time
when Dolores drifted off
with best man Bob
Alpha Beta Chi bro Bob
into the photo garden
with the twinkle lights and fountain
awash in spots of blue
and didn't return until it was time
to cut the cake and out

had distinctly designated Larry
the youngest for the toast
not Nat, not, not damned Nat
who, rising, awkward as a kiwi
skunk drunk, knocked over
baby brother's bubbly
onto the billiard green linen
only moments before crumbed

by the college kid who recalled
Larry from the bars
and was thinking about later
even though he had poli sci to cram for

which fizzed around the beef barley
or consommé, hot and fluffy popovers
Devonshire butter pats molded into swans
down Aunt Melody's de la Renta
down the bowed legs of the dais
Larry's spit-polished Doc Martens
onto the five-ply magenta carpet
Nat's feet were somehow planted in
glass raised high above his head
high above his plastered cowlick
towards the Lucite chandelier
an exact miniature
of Austria's gift to the Met

and rocking on the balls of his flat feet
said what Dolores would have said
if she had been there –
                nothing
a long, long longueur kind of nothing
a hush and blush big nothing

stretching all the way from
Great Neck to West Hempstead
from Anthony's Paradise & Catering
to kindergarten when Natty wet the floor
singing paw paws in the pocket
and trying to sidle from the glistening guilt

was caught by Miss Amelia
who made him a lesson
before she made him change

all the way back to Grandmother's Sun Club
when he tripped over her summer books
wrapped in brown bag jackets
and falling into the pool
came seconds close to drowning —
that slow sinking, that stillness, so sublime —
if not for the lifeguard
with the Chrysler spire tattoo
who fished him out and onto the concrete
(his knees still bore the scars)

all the way back to his attempted
first kiss on Abigail Gruenwald's
front porch, pale white light
heat lightning, the irascible urgings
of cicadas suddenly turning him
a seersuckered Tab Hunter
until a moth fluttered
between their pursed lips
and he bit the tip of her nose
(she too bore scars)

all the way back to yesterday
the day before and then some
a thousand and one slights
indignities, white lies
the evanescence of an uncorked mind

because with the extra dry martinis
and the South Beach knockout punch
the ratatouille pizzas and caviar egg rolls
with Larry's joint and Bob's parking lot line
he could not for the life of him
recall the name of the woman
in white sitting beside him
with the lower lip twitching
like a nun telling her beads
or a loser at Blackjack
when it's time to call it quits

because with the doe eyes and doughy skin
the dimple and the cheekbones
heavy with too much rouge
the only name he could think of was
Dolores, dear, devoted and dead
nor for that matter which brother
or cousin or high school / college buddy
was marrying again and why

and so Fat Nat said nothing
trying to smile the way
a pumpkin tries to smile
trying to look cool
the way a boy in black vinyl
tries hard looking kewl

until Larry, seizing the moment
sprung up like a radish, that quick
and red, whispered in his ear
what looked to the crowd like

Natty, be a good boy
or *Knock knee, please, enough joy*
and Uncle Jack the Second —
forever known as such
although no one could say why —
itching to show off his lindy prowess
to whatever blond tweens were around
bellowed something about cat tongues

and Nat seemed to grab hold
of some crumpled notion of propriety
taking out his glasses
from monogrammed pigskin
and carefully perching them
on the place his nose was permanently pinched
slowly unfolded a thrice folded sheet
from Anthony's Paradise & Catering
which unfortunately said nothing more than
Anthony's Paradise & Catering
and raised his empty glass up

up to the chandelier
synchronized to blink
to *We've Only Just Begun*
up to the Donna Summer disco ball
to the Tuscan tiled mansard roof
to Aquarius, to Scorpio, to Libra
to all the constellations of relatives and friends
and networking-is-important business colleagues

sitting agape as if watching
the first ooze of a mudslide
a Subaru sliding down an ice-glazed embankment
a Nature Channel jackal tackling a gazelle
and in his nasal phlegmy tenor –
no Richard Tucker him –
told the crowd to join him in a toast
join him in a toast to

Mary & Joseph, Abelard & Heloise, Ward & June,
George & Gracie, Pyramus & Thisbe, Albert & Victoria,

Bill & Hillary, Bonnie & Clyde, Rosalind & Orlando,
Viola & Orsino, Alice & Gertrude, Vita & Virginia,

Lunt & Fontaine, Maggie & Brick, Franklin & Eleanor,
Ferdinand & Isabella, Scarlet & Rhett, Robert & Clara,

Jackson & Lee, Nick & Nora, Ozzie & Harriet,
Donald & Daffy, Mary & Abe, Martin & Coretta,

Jack & Jackie, Abercrombie & Fitch, Lancelot & Guinevere,
Walt & Peter, Wystan & Chester, Charlie & Oona,

Dwight & Mamie, Nina & Nikita, Porgy & Bess,
Rick & Ilsa, Dante & Beatrice, Stanley & Stella,

Mimi & Rodolfo, Zelda & Scott, Nicholas & Alexandra,
Zelda & Dobie, Nora & Torvald, Archie & Veronica,

Tristan & Isolde, Catherine & Heathcliff, Oberon & Titania,
Homer & Marge, John & Yoko, Barbie & Ken,

Siegfried & Brunnhilde, Lola & Doc, Scylla & Charybdis,
Jason & Medea, Tarzan & Jane, Frida & Diego,

Abraham & Sarah, David & Bathsheba, Fibber McGee & Molly,
Blondie & Dagwood, Ricky & Lucy, Ralph & Alice,

Leander & Hero, Samson & Delilah, Zeus &Leda,
Zeus & Hera, Zeus & Niobe, Zeus & Europa,

Bert & Ernie, Fred & Wilma, Josephine & Napolean,
Romeo & Juliet, Mack & Mabel, Harold & Maude…

Paunchy Nat the older brother
hair slicked back with tonic
gut girded with Night Watch cummerbund
a deer in the headlights
with a tongue that keeps on running
a poet at the keyboard
afflicted with St. Vitus
a brain bilge stuck on backwash
finally halted by

blackout – drum roll –
spotlight – *shazzam*

a voice announcing
in bravissimo tones
The Real Star of the Evening
Anthony's World Famous Prime Rib

leaving Nat, sad Fat Nat
awkward as a kiwi, skunk drunk
alone in the dark
on the dais of the cosmos
blank paper and blank mind

believing as he must
in his moment of shamed triumph
that art and love
feed the same unlikely river
we swim by instinct upstream
against the drowning rapids –

that slow sinking, that stillness, so sublime –

and if we keep on keep on
keeping on through all
their astonishing and magical permutations
eventually – not this time
but the next time or the next –
we eventually might get it right

FROM THE CATALOGUES

Freud Carving Set In
Fitted Wooden Case
                Woodworker's Supply, Inc.

The same steel Sigmund used,
the original Viennese vanadium
once employed on Wolf Man, Rat Man, Anna O.
Durable tools which cut through tough complexes,
dig deep in any matter, whittle away
hard woulds, should-bes and blocks.

All professional pieces included –
straight chisels, gouges, V-parting tools, skews –
plus our eleven month selection boasts
an extra undercut knife, perfect
for August, absolutely free of charge.

The Freud Carving Set combines
the best of home workshop self-help
with classic, modern and post-gestalt designs.
No more clammy silence. No whiny discomposure.
No embarrassing splinters from ego or id.

Comes with fitted case
hewn from Sagaponack boxwood
and a heavy bolt in chelated tempered steel
to lock them up when everything else fails.

SCOTTISH OPERA

for Martie LaBare

There was too much flesh for the dress,
great globes of her protruding
from neck line and hem,
her pallor leached yet paler
by the sateen's black sheen.

In dim light, on a rattan reed stool,
she swung her legs above sawdust,
sipping the malt *me lad Mackay*
had handed her without smile or words.

In the Highland hamlet Durness
on the northwest coast of Scotland,
rendered by the Clearances
the most thinly populated stretch
in Western Europe, she sat alone

nursing her malt when the ancient oak
door opened and wind and rain and
a score of young men scrubbed ruddy
by the sea stormed into the pub.

Trays of pre-prepared sandwiches
were passed. Pints of stout and ale.
In their brogue-heavy chatter,
bits of discernable language emerged –
loch, laird, gloup, fook-ing Sutherlands –
like fast-fading strains of melody
when an orchestra warms up.

They ate. They drank. And within ten
they were gone. The girl, unacknowledged,
sat rigid with something like the tragic.
Costumed in the faded echo of a distant era,
neither Lady Macbeth nor Maria Stuarda,
the diva glared down disdainfully

at the snoopy creep crouched
in the corner with a fast pen in his hand,
the accidental audience of an *opera seria* –
historical, timeless, universal, local –
with a plot he couldn't start to ascertain.

STEPHEN DUCK

(1707 – 1756)

> *The trouble was that 18th century taste loved novelties…exemplified by the artificial hermitage complete with real hermit.*
>
> CHARLES ELLIOT, *Dead Trees and Fake Hermits*

The names of those who lost,
of course, are lost,
those who didn't make the cut
past first interview –
slow growing fingernails,
neat pate, pleasant grin.

Only the final choice
is known, plucked
from thresher tedium
the poet Stephen Duck
by Royal Appointment
of Her Majesty Queen Caroline
the Official Hermit of Richmond Park

who, ensconced in Merlin's Cave
and Hermitage, a beehive thatch
of rubble with gilt rails,
was given his charge,
to love God and disdain Man
while welcoming the visitors
steady as the rain.

A *memento mori* for the "moderns,"
surely Duck must have seen himself

like that, sitting with his housemates,
life-size wax figures of
the Wizard and Queen Bess,
dreaming in his low way
of awards and future residencies,
rejoicing for being the only
garden planting which could move.

And move he did,
becoming Yeoman of the Guard
rector of Byfleet, chaplain of Kew,
governor general of St. James Park.

How long he remained
in royal employ is not clear.
No scandal is recorded,
unlike the hermit of Pain's Hill
who despite a written contract
crept off nightly to a pub

(so hard it was to find
a decent hermit, some gentlemen
were reduced to staffing
with a stuffed one).

Capability Brown demolished
the Queen's folly
before the century was finished.
Rats ate the wax.
And as for Duck,
befriended and mocked
by the likes of Swift and Pope,
he took his poetry seriously
and drowned himself in the Thames.

ELEGY FOR POLLOCK

(1913 – 1956)

> *...painting is a state of being...*
> *Painting is self-discovery.*
> *Every artist paints what he is.*
>
> JACKSON POLLOCK, June, 1956

Jackson Pollock dead. His car,
green speeding Olds, had completed
the transaction, flung from
a slight curve, skidded and screeched
and crashed in a clump of small trees.

It was August. And the man was
dead. His wife was flying frantically
from Paris, thank you postcard
for red roses preceding her.
How are you, Jackson? she'd ventured

at the end, as if she needed answers.
Encased in guilt and plaster,
his final pretty fling slept drymouthed
in the hospital reliving the night's
wreck, as she would for years to come,

listen to tires on an oil grit road whine.
And dreaming, perhaps, better dramas
her own making, or the gaudy false
importance young accessories sometimes wear.
Yet the man was dead, he was dead

before that crackup / dead as his good
doctor, honest homespun Moses
who had parted the martinis and cleared
the way for work, who had carbonized
before him in a wreath of blasted steel.

Accidents? Well… The auto death
machine, bartered with his art,
lay a twisted ton of sculpture,
that medium he'd worshipped
though he'd made his way with line.

He'd come to the end of the line
some years before, said what he had
to say; there simply wasn't more. So…
abandoning method to imitation, abandoned
himself by the simple village savior

he had given in to rage.
Resumed drinking. Cracked his ankle.
Broke his leg. Stopped painting.
The dreams, maybe the dreams,
were the worst part of the leaving –

even the vacuum
became a dog, snapped and attacked.
Ahab, his living hound, howled
that evening at the moon, but she
so long embattled wasn't much surprised,

nor the neighborly sea, much surprised,
they had witnessed his self-
mourning. Soon his wife, back, scared,
crept into the house, watching out
for his mad ghost, began the hard

adjustment to a muscled widowhood.
And for us, the myth-eaters, as well,
the sorting out began for the real Paul
McCoy.* Lacking a helpful spirit to tap out
the addenda, we can only search and

search again the work. There
the *energy made visible*,** the life poured out,
emptied and perfected. And death,
the artist's death, a palpable completion
before that primal canvas void.

---

* Paul Jackson Pollock's father was born LeRoy McCoy and was adopted by the Pollock family at the age of two. Pollock dropped his first name when he came East to New York.

** The phrase *energy made visible* comes from B.H. Friedman's 1972 biography of the artist.

PARENTHESES

in memory of Isabella Gardner

Cradles for whispers and facts
separated cymbals, they qualify
(sometimes) elaborate (when necessary)
explain beyond the pure heart
of the matter. In another age
(a simpler age) we might have seen them
as hands blessing the day's bread,
cupping water or mid-clap
but are apt to see them now as desperate
hands extended (reaching but not touching)
trying to aching to (but failing)
or as circles whacked, incised.

One word fits inside (neatly)
but they also stretch (accommodating
all that we dare to give, words
of observation passion understanding
small important words like *sea* or *me*
the skin pulled tighter tighter)
until they snap back (small).

Although they serve us well
in framing our addenda
their best trait is breathless elasticity
(pliant enough to hold entire lives

TRAGEDY

for Aaron Fink & Anne Mastrangelo

Because the word seems vast
we blow it cold over frozen graves,
row after row of snow laden graves,
a wind which can't be counted
like a century's dark tears.

Or we break it down in decades –
the free rein of greed, sleeping psychosis
of swivel chair or park bench,
room upon room of disease,
the specific historical sense of generation.

But all of this is schooled
and we are always unschooled in tragedy.
It comes quickly and comes small –
the infant in his crib rattles once
and dies, as the grizzled wino dies

and the selfish stockbroker dies
and room upon room of my friends die
and the years fly by and die
and row upon row of slatted cribs go on –
we are all infants rattling eternity.

AFTER A PHONE CALL

After a phone call,
after a talk, after the news is known

you pull the sky tight over your head
and try to write a history of the sea –

not the events which happened upon,
movements of armadas, battles fought

and lost, fleets ironclad or rigged
tensed for eventful dawns,

which frigate sank which frigate
what schooner set sail to discover

technicolor lands, to prove the
earth was as round as pure greed,

not the course of luggers or xebecs,
barquentines, galeas, caravels or flutes

nor them that peopled
the sea, captains and cooks,

admirals and boatswains,
hirsute pirates with odd teeth,

the workers and the worked upon,
the revelers and reviled,

slim men in dhows
unfurling nets in Omani dawns,

penurious unfortunates dragooned
from the taverns of Stromness or Penzance,

people sick from their own stink
packed in the darkest of history's black holds,

nor the saga of the commerce of the sea,
maws filled with sugar or cars,

cuckoo clocks, oranges, isinglass, cloves,
sunflowers, paper, malachite, robes,

none of this is what you're after,
the busyness or business,

high jinx or expectations,
none of that interests you,

not at all,
no, because

after a phone call, after a talk,
after the news is known

what you want
is a history of the sea —

the blow by blow record
of each wave whipped by winds

great or small, the story of a droplet,
lifted skyward, making its way

from St. John to Connemara,
a minute by minute account of the tides,

the calibration of vortexes and races,
Corryvreckan, Swelkie, Merry Men of Mey,

the epic tale of ice melt
from Gaumukh to Bengal,

Geladaindong to Shanghai,
Lake Itasca to the dead zones of the Gulf,

salt water jazz with all its sax sexy riffs,
the funky musk of brackish ballads,

crushed chromium of heat light,
weightless slabs of dream slate,

the history of evaporation,
legacy of erosion,

the exact enumeration of brine
and all things briny,

the nono-bathymetrics
forty leagues from Fear,

because
after

a phone call, after a talk,
after the news is known,

what you want is the barter and
the promise, the back-dated

guarantee, the eternal
impossible, the whole of it, the all

even as you know that
remembering that one wave

that one day, rising in heavy July
which lobbed a gentle arc

and spangled his blond tousle
with an innocence so dewy

and beautiful it stang, the song of
the moment on his parched and salted lips,

that brief wave, that one wave,
in the long and impossible history of love

has to be enough, must be,
is enough

now, and how you
smile to recall.

Photograph © Jim Werkowski

PAUL GENEGA is the author of five chapbooks and four previous full-length collections of poetry, including Salmon's *That Fall: New and Selected Poems*. Over a thirty-plus year career, his poetry has garnered numerous awards, including The Lucille Medwick Award (New York Quarterly), Charles Angoff Award (The Literary Review), The "Discovery" Prize (The Nation) and The Allen Ginsberg Awards (Honorable Mention, The Paterson Literary Review). Nominated three times for a Pushcart Prize, he is also the recipient of an individual fellowship in poetry from the National Endowment for the Arts. He teaches at Bloomfield College, New Jersey, where he founded the creative writing program and currently serves as Chair of the Division of Humanities.